Winter Lightning

poems

Winter Lightning

poems

Kyle Doty

Apprentice House
Loyola University Maryland
Baltimore, Maryland

First Edition

Printed in the United States of America

Paperback ISBN: 978-1-62720-123-0
E-book ISBN: 978-1-62720-124-7

Design: Luisa Beguiristain
Editorial Development: Shannon O'Connor

Published by Apprentice House

Apprentice House
Loyola University Maryland
4501 N. Charles Street
Baltimore, MD 21210
410.617.5265 • 410.617.2198 (fax)
www.ApprenticeHouse.com
info@ApprenticeHouse.com

For Sharayah, again.
For Jada, Sariye, Liam, Ames, and Eero.

Acknowledgements

Thanks to Sarah Richardson, editor extraordinaire! I'm glad you crawled out of your box long enough to help on this project. Yours was a kind and unexpected friendship.

Thanks also to those who meet at the Robinson's house. I glean some of the most divine inspiration from you all. Keep going, never stop, and know that I love you all.

Skip and Beth Swiger, you stumbled into our lives for what you believed was a short stopover. Hahaha...little did you know you'd get stuck with us. This friendship has been galvanizing, and much of this project was encouraged by your love and support.

To the people I grew up with in Riverside and also those in Attica, thank you. The landscape and spirit of Fountain County runs deep in this book.

And once again, thanks to mom and dad for raising me where I could stretch out and grow as big as I wanted.

Several of these poems were first published in the following publications:

"Work Day" first appeared in *Stepping Stones Magazine*

"Blessingway" first appeared in *Screamin' Mamas Magazine*.

"Past Midnight" first appeared in *Third Wednesday*.

"Tonight We're Waiting" first appeared in *Helen Literary Magazine Blog*: Friday Night Specials.

Contents

Indianaland

*I first heard the term Indianaland from
childhood friend, Lauren Strasburg

Arrowhead

Crossing the dusty summertime field,
hot dirt like crumbs, not a few patches
of tangled, weedy grass, leftover corn stalks
from last year, and soybean remnants, I wander.

If anyone notices me from the one road
in and out of Riverside, my small body
will be a pale speck in the middle of the arid field.
My feet, which will one day tread the streets of Istanbul,
Comayagua, and Port-Au-Prince, sweaty in laced-up shoes,

leave marks in the soil, a trail of where I came from—
a modular home tucked away in the woods,
mom on the porch reading Danielle Steel,
laundry hanging on the line out back,
gnats swarming at the screen door—

I press forward, my childish feet one in front of the other.
This is the farthest I've been from home.
Not the farthest I'll be, because when adulthood comes,
I'll have to try and put myself at the edge of the world
every so often just to feel my pulse.

On the ground something catches my eye—
a smooth grey stone with ridges, an arrowhead.
Years ago some Indian boy tread this path barefoot,
probably cogitating about some girl back home
who will one day be his wife.

Perhaps he dropped his arrowhead while hunting deer or turkey;
just a boy, he's still responsible for dinner.
I pick it up and hold it in my radically pure palm and feel the weight of it,
the warmth of it from the sun.
I pocket it and turn around to head back home, because soon I'll run into the
    river and I'm not allowed to go that far alone.

Every year the Wabash claims at least one curious boy from the dry earth.

Hunting Mushrooms

Heat lightning flashes passively to the north.
My wife and kids have been asleep for
hours, and I'm up thinking about hunting mushrooms.

You begin at dawn, preferably after a
night of good rain, and it must be
cold enough to don a fleece jacket,
maybe a knit cap.

When we went, my dad and me,
grandpa always came along carrying
his walking stick. The only sounds
were the crunch of detritus underfoot
and grandpa's whistling.

Three generations walking equally spaced
apart looking under brush and rocks for
the miniature fungus that
later grandma would fry in bacon grease
and salt—a flavor combination, as a child,
I never liked.

While I was learning the finer points of
hunting mushrooms, grandpa's mind
had already begun to go.

Soon he misplaced things, ended up at
the store for batteries only to return with
cat food or the cap gun his son asked for
at Christmas forty years ago.

I wonder if the song he whistled in the woods
was a good memory, say, the tune
he and his sweetheart danced to at the lodge,
or if the tune and its place in time were out of reach.

Like this heat lightning tonight, I wonder
if that's like a memory—a silent spark that
one minute is there and the next
gone.

Indiana Fields, Summer Morning

Light screams from the round
of the sun.
Clothed in night, bathed in
crystal dew, fields yawn awake
and drink in the light,
throw themselves at the mercy
of the sun—worshippers confessing
their need. Begging pity, they
trust the sun, not to scorch,
but to sustain.

Poem: Nostalgia

Farmers abandon their barns for whatever reason
a person abandons a thing. The small barn near
our house, tucked away in the narrow strip of woods
that hugs the creek, had a tractor inside.
There was more ensepulchred there too: old tires, a spool
of wire, rusty tools.
There were a number of abandoned barns around
the small village. Each one frozen in time, the effluvia
of decaying wood and leaves and rodents thick inside.
What causes a person to leave a place to the custody
of time?
The brothers I never knew were older by the time I
came around; by the time I was coming of age,
they were long gone—each had his own green life outside of mine.
We were separated by the politics of adults, by the span of years.
After a thing's been neglected for so long,
does it make sense to disturb it or should
you leave it snug in the grip of time?
By now those barns are gone; weather and rot took
their toll. In their place the grass grows up new and
greener, a tree sprouts up, perhaps a new barn. The
land gets another chance to support something significant.

Riverside, Indiana

1.
The creek offers a deterrent from the mundane.
In Riverside it's pronounced crick.
Most days it's dry as a bone; sometimes after
heavy rains there's a trickle. Grandma warned
of flash floods.

Playing one second, and the next, a rumble like
a cruel work truck or thunder—water
crashing through the culvert taking me by surprise
and sweeping me down to the Wabash. My head crushed
against rocks, my limbs broken against trees,

my bloated body found by some farmer a few days
later while fishing with his boy.
Many cool nights I lay in bed
paralyzed with the cavernous sound
of fear ringing in my ears.

It gave me pause when I took a trek
down to the creek to look for buried treasure, or
arrowheads, or nightcrawlers under the
the cool stones.

It flooded only once.
Summer. The calm creek swelled spilling
rushing water over its banks.
Water rose to the door of dad's Ram.

Grandma's apologue came true:
Never trust the creek. Never trust water.

2.
Still a boy, I stand in the center of the yard,
a tennis ball in my hand, bored already with
summer's freedom, yet dreading school in
the fall. There's smoke coming from the creek;
grandpa's burning trash. He has no concerns

about the environment, he doesn't worry about
the ozone layer—he's likely never heard of
the ozone layer, and if he has, it's something
only democrats and gays give a shit about.
He comes up from his burning, unsteady on his feet,
and scans the yard. His light eyes pass over me once,
twice, and then he moves in my direction. Something
in him has changed, and I'm just old enough to understand
that it's no longer grandpa.
"What are you doin' here?" he asks. "You causin' trouble?"
He thinks I'm someone else. He doesn't call me his
little buddy anymore. He doesn't know my name.
He's angry. "Get on outta here!" he shouts. "Go on! I said get
outta here!"

3.
Summer is stifling. Brutal. The heat cascades
from a sapphire sky.
I stand on our deck and listen to the silence of
summer in the country. The sky above my head
is the same one in other places, places like
Germany and Russia, China and Cambodia—
life happens everywhere, even in places you
can't see.
It's so quiet I can almost hear the soft breathing
of corn in the fields wrapped around our house.
A soft exhale, a whistling inhale.
A neighbor boy comes cruising down our dirt
driveway on his bike motioning for me to get my
own Schwinn and join him.
We're two boys on the main road heading towards
Independence—both the one that comes with
adolescence and the small town on the other side
of the Wabash. Our mission: two Cokes to stall the heat.
We stop to spit over the side of the bridge and
count how long it takes to make a splash in the
muddy water. We talk about girls and the wonders
they'll hold for us sometime in the future.

4.

The neighbors had horses and chickens.
I'd feed them from my boy sized
palm, pure, the color of ecru cream.
Delicate red apple slices for the horses,
the flesh the color of the moon at harvest
and butternut colored grain for the chickens.
My payment was handfuls of bright
red strawberries picked straight
from the narrow patch and gobbled.
Later, when she came into some money, she bought
up all the land around ours, tried to create her
own farming empire. Boxed in, we packed up
and moved south to Florida.

Standing Beneath the Moon in the Early Morning

The half moon bolted to
indigo sky hangs like
a pale eye.

It looks cold and
alone.

I can't recall noticing
the moon when I
was a boy.

I didn't revere the
gauzy glow siphoned
through bare trees

around our home in
the woods

or the way its milky
light washed the
oak boards of the
deck

and filtered through
the windows of my
room casting ghostly

light across my
bed, across my
narrow body.

Winter
Lightning

Early Morning

While the sun struggles to clock
in for second shift, I stand on the patio,
one with the dark of early morning,
effacing the tender sleep which made
its home in me during the cradle of night.

I paint a picture in obsidian air,
my finger hovering in front of my
face. I paint my love: deep asleep,
soft skin under sheets, warm.
I paint a kiss. Desire unraveled.

I paint a bridge which spans the earth.
An interconnected path which lovers take,
motivated by need, to fall into one another's
arms, to kiss, to cry.

I paint a man standing alone in a field
called concupiscence, naked,
strong arms at his side, feet planted
firmly into the soft black earth,

one thousand trees bending under the
weight of passion. He looks toward the
horizon where the sun is pulling itself up
from somewhere half a world away,

his eyes concentrated on the color
of the sky, the way the light on the
earth lightens from dark to grey to
purple.

And soon his body is saturated
in the brilliance of morning.
I step back to view my work.
Satisfied, I turn toward the house, stepping
through the door frame, enveloped
by the safety of shadows.

Abandoned House

The grass has grown up nearly knee high
in some places. Out front the palms
dropped their coconuts long ago;
no one's been home to pry them open

for their meat, their milk. The man who
lived here left months before the woman.
She took the kids and moved on, not
bothering to think about the coconuts, the palms.

Around back the pool was left
half empty. Scum and
insects have taken over.
The porch door was left unlocked.

Inside it's like life just stopped:
A lone cup on the counter, dishes in the sink,
an afghan likely woven together by someone's
grandmother rests across a tattered sofa.

The sliding door opens with a tug,
and I peer inside, suddenly afraid. What
is it I expect to find? A lonely body? A
cool gust of wind carrying a whispered incantation?

I shut the door and let
myself out back—around the pool,
through the swinging gate, and back
onto the street where the mailbox
stands, its mouth gaping, empty.

As I continue my walk, I notice from
a distance that the roof is new and
the palms are pregnant again, and
I wonder if that had been a welcome
mat I saw at the front door.

And I Reached Out And Touched The Nest As If To Apologize

The hornet's nest with its
paper-thin walls the color of
ash sits precariously in
the tree outside the window.

What about this particular
tree outside the bedroom
window on the corner of

the house were they
drawn to? And how
come during the summer
didn't you

write to tell me about your
hornet problem and the
undue stress of not
being able to open your

window on cool summer
nights?

Of course, it's entirely possible
that the hornets weren't causing
any trouble at all—
the light from the bedroom

and the hum of voices
kept them awake at night.
The discussions about hornets,
prejudiced complaints, signaled

it was time to go.

They took flight, abandoned home,
and rooted in another tree

in a quiet wood unencumbered
by noisy neighbors and

light pollution from the city.

for Nathan and Katie

At Dusk, Florida

Frystra transuding from
the pores of the radio—

Light from the bulb of the
sun a flare that cuts through
the gossamer humidity—

Somewhere from where
my ancestors got their
start, the sable sky snaps
and contracts like a July
glow stick and turns varying
shades of refulgent dawn.

Evening Notes

No deep growl of thunder tonight
or siren of lightning. Only mosquitos
and cicadas, and crickets. Just like when
I was growing up in Indiana—
the sun would sink lazily below
the horizon pulling up the yawning
moon from someplace across the
world, and we'd be on the porch
braving summer's humidity and listening
to the chorus of bugs out in the yard
and in the fields, reminding us that no
matter how small you are there's
importance in being.

The kitchen is quiet tonight.
Dishes have been washed, table cleaned,
only the hum of the refrigerator, standing
like a sentry, fills the room. I imagine a
mouse scurrying across the wood floor or
the faucet dripping, keeping time like
my aunt's grandfather clock that fascinated me as a boy.
A friend at the door, arms full of wine and flowers,
would be welcome. But then my poem writing would
end, and I'd not be able to think about how my
summer foreign students have taught me
how modest my life is. How the world is so
large with life in every corner, that teenagers
from anywhere are the same—they all want
validation and to find someone to love.

Back in Riverside when I was young and the
storms rolled in across the stretches of ecru
fields during summer, I'd lie in bed—my
small body hardly leaving an imprint in
the mattress—and mull over and over the
people across the earth just waking up and
wonder, if by some psychic connection,
they could feel our minds melded together
or if they felt they were being watched.

How to Tie a Bow Tie

Attached to my bathroom mirror is a
card with instructions for tying a bow tie
printed neatly with pictures –
small hieroglyphics indicating how to
tie the knot perfectly so that one side,
when pulled, tightens and the other side,
when pulled, loosens.
All this to look distinguished.
Every day I study
the pictures while washing my hands,
brushing my teeth, even though I've learned
the way all gentlemen should properly
tie the convoluted knot.
I didn't consult the card for my education.
A friend came by and showed me the whole
process in front of the mirror. But I can't part
with the card, from some department store,
because it stands for something now – life and
its complexities. Like why in the 21st century
I still must rinse the dishes before loading
the dishwasher, or why the children always seem
surprised when time comes for bed or picking
up their socks.
Tying a bow tie is a lot like life.
The whole thing seems so intricate until
someone shows you how, one night
when there's music, Olafur Arnalds probably, and
wine. Then you discover that it's not all that
complicated as long as that person,
a friend or lover, perhaps both, holds your
hand and leads you through it –
the end result is the same.
Either way you wind up with the bow tie unfurled
over your shoulders and staring into the countenance of the
moon with the exasperated look of wonder
on your face.

for James Buonocore

Inventory of my Desk Drawer

Tide pen, ruler, sleek black paper clips;
a few rubber bands, a pay stub;
staples, push pins, a birthday card, its
contents emptied, the note inside
forgotten.
A pair of earrings, twenty-six cents, a
box of crayons, colored pencils, markers,
highlighters; a broken pencil sharpener.
The leftovers of a school year;
   impotent remains of academic progress.

Elegy for the Dead

Light you respired.
Filling your body
with brilliant white,
the light you took in a ball like fire
tucked into your core—
mystics would call it your soul, the
Egyptians your Ib because it pulsates
brighter　　　　brighter
never dimming but brighter
than ten thousand stars
hanging above your head
until your body is enveloped
in the veil of light and
your secret interior a luminous
pearl.

First Day of Hurricane Season
June 1, 2014

Today marks the first day of
the new hurricane season –

Nothing's churning out in
the womb of the Atlantic,
nothing but a squall in the Gulf –

but that's all a storm needs:
a squall to get itself turned
around and agitated about
something, to turn in
on itself and ripsaw a path
toward land – perhaps a

channel right into Tropicalia.

For this, too, is the world - In response to Mary Oliver's "October"

For this, too, is the world:
The small concrete home inhabited by the mother with four
children from four separate, abandoning fathers. Each child
conceived in the hot, bare bedroom; each child the substitution
for a rent check.

The girl, fourteen, unable to distinguish between the lusty
eyes of desire and the soft embrace of romance.
Alone in the school bathroom, back against the tiled wall, still naked
and scared and cold, the boy she'd committed to gone, back to the dance,
back to his buddies.

For this, too, is the world:
The woman with the handsome man, the dream man, the man
she tells her friends about, the man she hints at possibly being **the one**,
sucking air, gasping at the intensity of their intimacy.

The man, the dream man, black sports car, expensive
house on the river, concentrating between pleasure and not
calling out the name of his boyfriend across town.

For this, too, is the world:
The clergyman sad and tired.
The bored child.
The man who walks alone in the rain.
The lady who goes home to nobody:
no kids, no husband, no lover.
The old couple sitting together in front of the blue flickering
screen wondering what the hell happened, they were just
seventeen.

For this, too, is life:
The young ones at the beach,
in the sun, playing, strutting. The
boys flexing, trying to get kissed.

The newlyweds in front of the mirror admiring
the growing belly, the smash of cells sticking together,
forming the first meaningful creation of their union.

For this, too, is life:
The divine drama in the pluck of stars,
in the naked place of darkness, where
no man can fathom the transparency of light;
every human emotion heightened, sensitive,
aware of one thing:
life in all its tragedy & promise rests on the
head of a pin, rests in the blink and breath
of earth and always,
it's always called joy.

Fort Myers Beach, June 2014

        Sunlight screams from the cerulean
sky washing the violated beach in Ultra
Violet rays –
There are hundreds here. All like religious
nomads making their pilgrimage to the gulf to
worship Ra the way their
ancestors did a thousand years ago in another
brutal land. They cooked meat
on open spits and bathed in the
saline water.
We don't have an intimate bond
with our food; we eat meat from
clear clean packages. Rather than
bathing, we splash and relax in the
warm tropical water.
Some bring their dogs led by leash to
experience the sanctity of
water, sun, sticky salt, gritty sand.

Morning Thunderstorm, June 13, 2014

I woke up to the sky proclaiming
its personality the way an adolescent
stands her ground –

this is who I am.
No rain, just noise.

Already my
body was hot, the sticky morning
crept in through the scores of cracks
and crevices in this old house.

I heard birds,
Sparrows maybe, the ones who
swoop and attack the cat and then
screech – a bird's cackle.
The birds were nose-diving &

play-fighting in
the trees, on the phone wires, as
if to say to the approaching storm
You can't get me! You can't get me!

Just the way children sing
it at the playground.

No wind this morning;
everything's still except those birds

and the chimes which
reach out and touch the other as if to say

Are you there? The way humans do,
going so long without touching,

talking, loving, that finally they'll

touch & love anyone, anywhere.

The rain comes in sheets –
like a curtain,
a veiled bride marching

toward her lover, toward the
consummation of her wedding –

it ravishes my body as I sit
in my wooden chair and write.

Past Midnight

It's after midnight and I'm here,
up, sipping tea and listening to the
sleeping dog huff and whine.

The scratching my pen makes against this
notebook would sound to a stranger like
I'm writing an urgent letter, say, to a lover—

telling her goodbye, that it was worth a shot.
Sometimes things don't last.
But there is no one else here except me

and the dog.
Unless you count the hundred or so people
flying above us in the airplane that just went over,

the deep hum, low rumble of twin engines.
They're folding up their newspapers, straightening
their hair and clothes after their in-flight nap,

peering down through their windows
and wondering what my light is doing on at
this hour and considering, perhaps, that

I'm just another one not getting enough rest
tonight. They're probably not even aware
that I'm writing a poem about them.

How we're connected now in a
strangely intimate way.

Red sky before snow

I'm told it's a saying.
One passed down from
adult to offspring beginning
sometime in history
when we made our homes
in caverns and work
was intimate with the
land.

Not like today where
work is sedentary and men
with manicured hands don't
know the feel of proper tools
against their palms.

I stand in the backyard
holding the sagging trash
bag, staring into the
dark sky with a crimson
hue, and think about the
men who first discovered
the red sky-snow pattern.

They could be my ancestors—
their blood passed down
father to son, father to son
until here I stand considering
the most profound discovery
of those men's lives.

Saturday Morning

Naked I came from my mother's womb
and naked I arose from my soft bed this
morning before the sun's light
etched away the stain of night.

I stood outside the door in the sprinkling
rain waiting for Inu to go – she stood
faithfully at my side refusing to wander

out, snout to ground, hunting for the
bathroom.
I heard a week or so ago that it's not

a fear of wet paws that makes dogs
act strange in the rain.
It's the sound of rain against the earth
that bothers them.

It hurts their ears.

Even though the sun was nearly on the horizon
and I wasn't tired anymore, I went back to bed
and burrowed deep under the soft pile of blankets.
The raw of my body snuggled against
the warmth of my Love's.
How long I lay there, nestled and warm,
listening to her soft breath, taking her in
through every sense but sight, nestled
and warm, I don't know.

Some things can't be measured.

The room turned grey and then
light. The rain pelting the roof
kept on and then stopped sometime
before the kids woke up.

Simple Atrocities

are the moon waning in the night sky,
the sun peeking its bovine head above
the horizon and rain
skirting around Tropicalia—

A simple grey sky is a
clean slate.
Grey is a starting over.

But I have it good.
Other atrocities in the world
are vicious:

Somewhere in Thailand there's
a young girl lying in bed
hoping the fat American man
with wads of cash has packed
up and gone,
hoping he's left the right amount
on the nightstand.

In Darfur a young man must
decide between his family
and the rebels pushing him
to join them,
either option will end in
slavery, and eventually, death.

Somewhere in Florida
Jeb Bush eyes the White House.
Donald Trump sketches the plans
for a wall.

The Graveyard Behind the House

I heard he was an abolitionist
and not a soldier. His headstone
a song for those buried there:
your life mattered, you fought and
were brave.

I was told the graveyard is for
black soldiers who fought in the Civil War.

Looking around the quiet suburban
landscape, I can imagine an ancient
war being fought here.

Men in grey uniforms and dirty forage caps
climbing the graveyard hill. Did any of
them feel the spongy pressure or hear the
footfalls over their heads—the foreshadowment
of what the place would be for them?

Outside the small kitchen window
David Cassel's headstone stands tall and
encourages twenty-first century citizens
who have never tasted war or served
in an army or experienced persecution:
"Death is but to sleep in Jesus
when this life is o'er."

Two days after Thanksgiving 11.29.14

I sit in the solitude of the warm afternoon light streaming in through the three
    windows.
The only breaks in the silence are the wind chimes out front and the cat
who must declare his presence upon entering through the open front door.

Pine fills the house with its sweet, masculine scent from the tree we put up last
    night
and decorated this morning.

I sit, one with the world, bathed in warm light.
What if by some tragic chance
I'm left alone without love?
Would I continue to pray? To praise? To be thankful?

The cat on the sofa doesn't think of these things.
He only washes his feet and perks up his pointed ears each time a car
crawls by the house or when the dog shifts herself around on her bed across

the room. The cat doesn't ask: what is my life?
The cat only knows he's here and that it's now.

Thursday Morning in the Adirondack Chair

Five hundred years ago there was
still inspiration to be found in a
freshly bisected orange, one hemisphere
wobbling on some bare wooden table.
Simplicity sparks light inside mankind.
Perhaps even my own ancestors found
themselves provoked by the intrinsic beauty of that light.
But then again, there's The Last Supper and
the tangled relationship between Jesus and Judas
taking place in front of our eyes, the spread of
untouched food, the wine, the anxiety among
the disciples—who among them is greatest?
Or all those water lilies floating untouched by anything
other than the breeze and warm sun.
There's the capacious sky in Starry Night.
None of those an ode to simplicity.
Unless they are and that bisected orange, the one
hemisphere still now, is like a port to some
foreign dimension of light where the more
byzantine ideas come from.

Winter's Signal

Today the wind blows swift and
cool from the North,
carrying winter's kiss,
making the chimes out front dance
and sing their joyful song.

Halloween last night was cool.
The kids didn't shed their costumes
early, whining it was too hot.
The only ones out, just the seven
of them,
Halloweening in the neighborhood by
the river,
they brought in a haul.

Time change tonight signals
winter's coming, as though
the gusty wind now doesn't
foreshadow the same.
I've looked forward to right now
since late June –

sitting in the tree swing,
sweating, longing for the
season change
thanking God for hope
        for better days.

Not Stating the Obvious

The first day of hurricane season was a week ago—
last night to the east was a rainbow, the west a
tornado funnel.

I don't want to do the obvious and parallel
the significance of the two events that life
is similar, both inspiring and ominous, two paths that diverge,

one choice over another could amend
your course.

I don't want to do that. You're too smart
for that. You'll see right through my dime store analysis.

Opening coconuts with a drill, a hammer –

my ancestors used crude tools,
brute strength.
     I'm contemporary with modern
solutions to ancient quandaries.
While I drill, my children watch
on with starlit wonder —
     their daddy's using tools –
a small miracle in and of itself.
My father can use tools as
if they're extensions of his own
beat up hands – a knack I did not
pick up.
I became an academic.
The drill opens a hole in
the hard green shell, splashing
me with water.
The meat is slimy
and tastes bad.
     The kids love it.
I think about my summer in Panama
when I was younger, living with the Kuna
on the edge of the Darien – a Native
shimmied up a tree with a machete
and brought back coconuts
he hacked in two with one grunt—
     skills I'll never possess.

Midsummer

Since May, when our friend's baby died,
anything lugubrious steals away my breath.

This year's been hard on feeling.
It seems as though someone's turned up
the volume and stepped away
from the controls leaving no one brave enough
or sensible enough to turn it down.

The twins were a lambent jot on the
landscape these past few months;
told they'd be too small, that they'd
struggle—they were born strong and sure.

Tonight at the funeral for the daughter of
a friend, I couldn't help thinking how unfair
it is that this family has eulogized two of
their children.

What struck me was their faith—
it never seemed to waver.
At home behind closed doors
they may have shouted and cursed,
thrown things, broken down; they may
have been rightfully angry at the Divine.
But tonight they sang of God's kindness and
goodness and mercy—they preached grace.
And I suppose they're right.

On the beach one evening we stood and
watched the sun sink below the stretch
of interminable horizon. With a silent
pop the blazing orb disappeared, and I
couldn't help but imagine it rising like
a god and shining on some foreign
people I've never met clear across
the earth.

Winter Lightning

Rain, winter lightning that stretches its voltaic fingers
across the cimmerian sky, slow roll of thunder a proclamation—
angels with trumpets.
The highway is congested tonight;
      beams of light from other cars like phantom eyes
charge northward.
Our car is in the pack forging forward like some long-snouted animal.

Winter lightning crawls across the sky again,
reminding me of the way an idea sparks, the way
love jolts the body, the mind—
      the slow crawl of electric light folds in on itself,
and my inspiration lingers for the rest of the journey.

Birth

Attention Deficit Disorder

By lamplight I scribble my pen
across the paper in my now
year-old notebook.

It's still out tonight; the
dark crept in quickly due
to the all day cloud cover.

A storm is brewing some two
thousand miles away, dividing
our attention now between

our modern lives and the slow
turn of what would be only a
thunderstorm if it were found

someplace like Nebraska. The
small tangle of storms in the
Atlantic is not unlike the way

human life is formed sometime
after love –
something my wife tells me

she wants. Now my attention is
split again until I'm unsure I'm
able to focus on any one thing at all.

New Beginnings

Our friends to the north tell us of
the wonders of fall:
a feeling in the air that the
season is changing; a time to
reflect on the past and plan
the future –
new beginnings are upon them.

New beginnings are here, too.
Another storm is curling and taking
shape in the Caribbean at the same time
tiny cells are forming into life inside
the cradle of my wife's womb.

Soon our lives will change, again;
change that lasts for the next whatever
years. Sleepy newborn wrestling the
night; diapers; standing then
toddling then walking; first foods;
first sleepover; first love; then it'll be
over, poof, and Sharayah and I will
be standing, arms around each other
on the front porch, waving goodbye
to a piece of our hearts.
"It was so good," I'll say.
We'll head inside and I'll make some
tea and she'll paint something and
the house will be all too quiet.

Women

A spark of light ignites
life inside of you

you hold the power of
existence within your
frame

without you life would
expire.

What is it like to be life for another life?

Expecting

The zygotic scribble that planted itself
deep inside my wife's body
turned out to be gemelos. Both boys.

Each one smaller than a
homegrown turnip. Today
they lie in the shape of

the number seven. Tomorrow
maybe they'll interpret zero
or two.

Blessingway

The women are a tribe.
Mystics crowded around my wife,
crowded around the bed where
the twins first sparked to
life.

Each woman a world all her own,
not boasting the power she
possesses—a womb, an instinct,
the ability to tuck life away inside her life.

It's sacred.
This is more than the celebration
of life and birth and forthcoming life.

This is a birthright.
This is spiritual.

One woman paints henna
on my wife's belly, the others
hand her stones, each one found
to represent her courage, her beauty,
her spirit. All different shapes,
all small but with noticeable weight
when held in the center of the palm.

The babies kick and the women
chuckle, nod approvingly.
They have affirmed this life now
and have called it good.

Work Day

Up early, still dark, the light
from the sun's body hasn't
crested the edge of the horizon
yet.
I'm dressed, coffee in hand,
waiting for the morning grey to
wash out the remaining black
of night.
Any day now we could have twins,
Ames and Eero,
boys my wife dreamed of years
ago just now becoming a reality.
My wife, she's asleep in the room,
having finally drifted off after
another fitful night—the norm for all
of her pregnancies.
I stand in the bright kitchen holding my
coffee cup, looking out the window
at the just now lightening sky.
On agenda for today: teach memoir
and grade one more set of essays.
My wife will stay home and grow
babies and love the other children.
She'll spend hours just feeling the
boys kick and wrestle through the
thick membrane just beneath her skin.

Tonight We're Waiting

for labor to start.
My grandmother always told me
"a watched pot never boils."
Maybe my grandmother was right.

The dog is a pile at the
foot of the bed—soft snores escaping
her short snout—she waits along with us.
She was never a mother, has grey-washed
memories of being a puppy,
but she still has primal instincts.

She rests at our feet only looking
up occasionally to check on us as
if she's offering the best advice she
knows: they'll come when it's time.

About the Author

Kyle Doty is the author of *Hush, Don't Tell Nobody*. He attends Arkansas State University where he is pursuing his Master's in Education Theory and Practice. He is also a student at Cana New Wine Seminary where he is deepening his knowledge of scandalous grace. He lives in Florida with his family and works as a middle grades educator. Go to kyledoty.com to learn more about the author and his work. If interested in his theological work, you can learn more at Songlifestyle.com

Apprentice House is the country's only campus-based, student-staffed book publishing company. Directed by professors and industry professionals, it is a nonprofit activity of the Communication Department at Loyola University Maryland.

Using state-of-the-art technology and an experiential learning model of education, Apprentice House publishes books in untraditional ways. This dual responsibility as publishers and educators creates an unprecedented collaborative environment among faculty and students, while teaching tomorrow's editors, designers, and marketers.

Outside of class, progress on book projects is carried forth by the AH Book Publishing Club, a co-curricular campus organization supported by Loyola University Maryland's Office of Student Activities.

Eclectic and provocative, Apprentice House titles intend to entertain as well as spark dialogue on a variety of topics. Financial contributions to sustain the press's work are welcomed. Contributions are tax deductible to the fullest extent allowed by the IRS.

To learn more about Apprentice House books or to obtain submission guidelines, please visit www.apprenticehouse.com.

Apprentice House
Communication Department
Loyola University Maryland
4501 N. Charles Street
Baltimore, MD 21210
Ph: 410-617-5265 • Fax: 410-617-2198
info@apprenticehouse.com • www.apprenticehouse.co

www.ingramcontent.com/pod-product-compliance
Lightning Source LLC
Chambersburg PA
CBHW051739040426
42447CB00008B/1209